MW01608700

THE BRITISH MUSEUM

JOHN JULIUS NORWICH

WELCOME to the British Museum. It is, as you can see, an enormous building, and many people visiting it for the first time find it daunting. But though we can't make the Museum any smaller, we can make it easier to understand; and that is the real purpose of this guide

Each of the tours described here will give you a rich experience of the museum's collections. They can all be fitted into a morning but you may prefer to linger over one and return another day.

The Museum has a rolling programme of renewing its galleries, so we do apologise if any of the rooms mentioned are not open during your visit.

Top left. Bronze shield from Moel Siabod, Gwynedd, *c.* 1100-900 BC.
Centre. Wooden coffin-lid of Pasenhor. Egypt, 22nd Dynasty, *c.* 850 BC
Below. Detail of an Assyrian relief from Nimrud, *c.* 865 BC.

1. The Ancient World

Turn sharp left immediately inside the Main Entrance, go through the Bookshop, then through the first opening on your right into what is known as the Assyrian Transept. Spare only a quick glance at those two huge monsters on your left – for we shall be returning to Assyria later – and pass straight into the world of the Pharaohs.

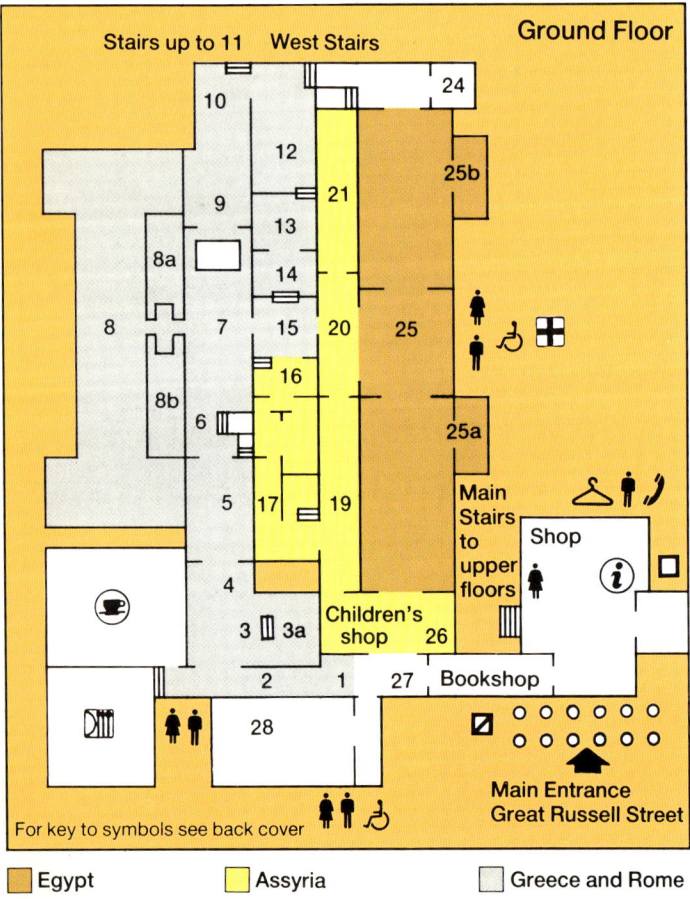

Ground Floor

Stairs up to 11   West Stairs

10
12
9
13
14
8a
8
7   15   20   25
8b
16
6
25a
5   17   19
Main Stairs to upper floors
Shop
4
3   3a   Children's shop   26
2   1   27   Bookshop

28

Main Entrance
Great Russell Street

For key to symbols see back cover

24
25b

■ Egypt   ■ Assyria   ■ Greece and Rome

N.B. Galleries may be rearranged from time to time, and objects removed on loan or for conservation.

Ancient Egypt

[25] We enter the Egyptian Gallery between two black granite seated statues of one of the great builders of ancient Egypt, **King Amenophis III,** who reigned from 1417 to 1379 BC. Just behind the left heel of the larger one you will see carved the name BELZONI. G.B. Belzoni was an extraordinary Italian who, having once earned his living as a strong man at London fairs, was responsible for moving several of the heaviest Egyptian statues (including the giant head of Ramesses II which you will see farther on) from their original sites to the banks of the Nile, from where they were shipped to London – no mean achievement in the case of objects weighing seven or eight tons. Behind this statue and to the left we come to one of the few items on the tour which is not a work of art as such: the famous **Rosetta Stone,** found in 1799 by Napoleon's soldiers in the Nile delta. The inscription on the stone is relatively unremarkable in itself: a fairly run-of-the-mill

The Rosetta Stone

decree given out in 196 BC by the priests of Memphis. What makes the stone so important is the fact that the text is written in three scripts and two languages: Egyptian hieroglyphs at the top, then Egyptian demotic script, and finally Greek. At the time of its discovery the two Egyptian scripts were undeciphered, but thanks partly to the presence of the Greek version and as a result of over twenty years' painstaking detective work by several brilliant scholars – notably the Frenchman J.F. Champollion – the key to them was found at last and the long-lost secrets of a vanished civilisation were finally revealed.

A little farther along on the right you will see a doorway which gives on to a long narrow gallery running parallel to the main one. Enter it and turn left. You immediately come upon a most arresting head of painted sandstone, with wide, staring eyes and wearing a high white crown. This is **King Mentuhotpe II** (2060-2010 BC), founder of the Egyptian Middle Kingdom; he appears again in a painted limestone relief on the wall to the left. At the end of this side gallery is another marvellous **head,** carved this time in green schist, very different in style but every bit as haunting as the other. In contrast to the almost trembling alertness of Mentuhotpe, this face has all the impassivity of an oriental Buddha, serene and inscrutable to the point where it loses all sexual characteristics: scholars are still debating whether it represents the great Queen Hatshepsut (c.1503-1482 BC) or her co-regent and successor, King Tuthmosis III (c.1504-1450 BC).

Before leaving the side gallery, don't on any account miss the glorious **tomb painting from Thebes** on the end wall. Dating from about 1400 BC, it shows a nobleman named Nebamun out in the marshes hunting wildfowl, accompanied by his somewhat

Painted sandstone head of Mentuhotpe II, 11th Dynasty, c.2025 BC, and a royal head in green schist, 18th Dynasty, c.1490 BC.

Nebamun hunting in the marshes. Tomb-painting from Thebes, 18th Dynasty, c.1400 BC.

overdressed wife, his distinctly underdressed daughter and his cat. In his right hand he clutches three decoy herons: meanwhile, all the live birds around are in a state of panic – not surprisingly, since the cat has already captured three of them. For liveliness, humour and brilliance of observation, there are few Egyptian paintings anywhere that can match this.

Return down the side gallery, take the second opening to the right and return to the main room. There you will see facing you three life-size granite statues of **King Sesostris III** (1878-1843 BC).

The best is the one on the right. Here is something quite different from anything we have seen so far. The previous faces have all conformed to the religious conventions of the day; now at last we are looking at a real person – a proud, unbending man with a down-turned mouth and huge bat ears. We should recognise him anywhere.

Now walk slowly along the gallery, passing down the centuries as you go, and pause at the gigantic speckled granite head of **King Amenophis III,** his arm laid neatly alongside him. (The crowned head is nearly 3 m high; if the whole statue were here it would go right through the roof.) To the left of the head is a group of four figures – two seated and two standing – of the **lioness goddess Sakhmet;** and next to them, between the two columns, one of the most appealing groups in the whole Museum – a curiously touching **man and wife,** seated side by side and holding hands, looking out with serene confidence into eternity.

Left to right.
Head of a colossal red granite statue of Amenophis III, from Karnak. 18th Dynasty, *c.*1390 BC.

Gilded inner coffin of Henutmehit. 19th Dynasty, *c.*1290 BC.

Limestone pair-statue of a man and his wife. 18th Dynasty, *c.*1350 BC.

Black granite statue of Sesostris III. 12th Dynasty, *c.*1850 BC.

Ramesses II: head from a colossal granite statue. 19th Dynasty, *c.*1270 BC.

and lived to be nearly 100. Look how cunningly the sculptor has chosen a block of two-colour granite, using it to differentiate the head from the body; look, too, at the sheer breadth of those massive shoulders. (The hole in the right one was drilled by French soldiers in an early effort to remove the statue; they failed, but Belzoni managed it a few years later, in 1816.) Just beyond Ramesses, to the right, take the entrance to another side gallery. The doorway dramatically frames the beautiful gilded inner coffin of a lady called **Henutmehit,** who was a priestess of the god Amun during Ramesses' reign. (Her outer coffin is in Room 61 upstairs, with more of the Egyptian collection.) Had the coffin remained hidden as intended, this dazzling work of art would never have been seen again after Henutmehit's death.

In the first wall-case to the left is a memorable seated figure of **Iti,** an official of around 700 BC, wearing a curious double wig; and, further along towards the end, the huge **sarcophagus** of the Memphite priest Nesisut, with a religious procession carved along its sides and a figure of the goddess Isis, kneeling with wings outstretched, on the end of its lid You should also spare a glance for the case against the end wall, which contains a statue of the hawk-headed god **Horus** as a Roman emperor and, next to him, a golden-headed and remarkably well-endowed **baboon.**

Back in the main gallery, walk to the end, where there is a choice. If you have the time and the energy, climb the stairs to the Egyptian rooms above (Rooms 60-66), where there are mummies and mummy-cases in abundance, to say nothing of 'Ginger' in Room 64 – a 5,000-year-old corpse, not mummified but dried naturally in the sand. Alternatively, turn sharp left through the glass doors and return to the Assyrian Transept by the narrow corridor running parallel to the Egyptian Gallery. This brings you face to face with a completely different civilisation.

Bronze cat, sacred to Bastet, with gold nose-ring and earrings. Roman Period, after 30 BC. *Right.* Cat mummy from Abydos. Roman Period, after 30 BC (Room 60, upper floor).

They mark the entrance to the Central Saloon, where the larger statues are grouped around the edge, with smaller objects in the central glass cases. Among these be careful not to miss, first (in the left-hand case) that most majestic **cat,** representative of the goddess Bastet, with its gold nose-ring and earrings and a silvered amulet hanging from its neck; and (in the case on the right) a tiny **hippo,** his blue-glazed body painted with aquatic plants.

The northern continuation of the gallery is dominated by the huge head of **King Ramesses II,** traditionally the pharaoh of the Exodus, who reigned from 1304 to 1237 BC, had 150 children

Glazed composition hippopotamus decorated with aquatic plants. Middle Kingdom, c.1900 BC.

Ancient Assyria

In the 7th century BC, the vast Assyrian Empire stretched from Egypt to Iran, from ancient Asia Minor to the deserts of Arabia. A succession of royal palaces has been excavated at three principal sites – Nineveh and Nimrud on the Upper Tigris and Khorsabad a little farther north.

21 Room 21, the first Assyrian gallery, is given over to **reliefs** from the reigns of King Ashurbanipal (668-627 BC) and his grandfather Sennacherib (704-681 BC) at Nineveh, the best of which is the splendid set-piece at the end on the right, illustrating the **campaign in South Iraq.**

Human-headed winged bull from Khorsabad, *c.*710 BC.
Below. The battle of Til-Tuba (detail). Relief from Nineveh, *c.*660-650 BC.

This gallery leads into an open hall (Room 20) with more reliefs and, on the right, a room (16) dominated by two huge **human-headed bulls** similar to the lions in the Assyrian Transept. Like those, they have been given five legs, placed so that they appear to be stationary when seen from the front, but in motion to anyone looking at them from the side.

Next to the bulls is a small staircase: descend it if you like, and on the floor below you will be rewarded by more superb reliefs from Nineveh. You should then on no account miss, in Room 89, the magnificent racing camel on the dividing wall; nor the Battle of Til-Tuba on the end wall; nor, in Room 88a, a remarkable representation of locust kebabs.

19 Returning upstairs and continuing past another pair of monsters standing guard at the entrance to Room 19, we find ourselves among the reliefs from the palace of King Ashurnasirpal II (883-859 BC) at Nimrud. Near the entrance, on the left, is a fine stone **panel of the king** himself, enthroned among his attendants; on the right are fascinating **scenes of battle and the chase,** including a delightful depiction of soldiers escaping across a river, using inflated goatskins like water-wings. In the centre of this room you will see the famous **Black Obelisk of Shalmaneser III** (858-824 BC), one side of which shows foreign rulers – including Jehu, King of Israel – bringing tribute.

17 Superb scenes of **lion hunts** featuring King Ashurbanipal can be found in Room 17, just before the end of the corridor to the right. Panels in the adjacent Lachish Room show the capture of the Biblical city of Lachish in Judah by King Sennacherib in 701 BC.

Leave Room 19 at the far end, turn left, and you are back in the Assyrian Transept. Round to the right is the entrance to Room 1: your introduction to the world of classical antiquity.

Top left. Assyrian troops pursuing Arabs on camels. Detail of a relief from Nineveh, *c*.645 BC.

Left centre. Grooming a horse: detail of a relief from Nimrud, *c*.865 BC.

Left below. Men bringing tribute to the Assyrian king. Scene from the Black Obelisk of Shalmaneser III, from Nimrud, *c*.825 BC.

Right. Ashurbanipal killing a lion. Detail of a relief from Nineveh, *c*.645 BC.

Right below. Reconstruction by A.H. Layard of Ashurnasirpal's throne-room at Nimrud, showing how the reliefs may have looked when painted.

Greece and Rome

Pass through the first two rooms – devoted respectively to the early Cycladic civilisation and to the Bronze Age and Geometric Period, including Minoan Crete and Mycenae – and turn right into Room 3 (Archaic Greece).

3 Greek painting and sculpture during the Archaic Period (before *c*.550 BC) has a marvellous springtime freshness about it, in contrast to the austerities of the Geometric Period which preceded it. Just look at the Athenian **black-figured vases** in the long central case, and in particular at the beautiful amphora showing **Achilles** about to kill the Amazon queen Penthesilea; turn round, and in the case behind you you will see a **bronze helmet** almost indistinguishable from the one he is wearing.

5 Around 530 BC red-figured vase-painting, where the backgrounds were painted instead of the figures, came into fashion. In their inventiveness, imaginative power and sheer *brio* the **red-figured vases** from the 5th-century Golden Age of Ancient Greece are, if anything, even lovelier than their black-figured predecessors. At about the same time the white-ground technique was invented, an exquisite example of which can be seen in a case half-way along Room 5: a drinking cup showing the goddess **Aphrodite riding a goose.** This room also contains remarkable reliefs from the so-called **Harpy Tomb** (*c*.480 BC) at Xanthos in Lycia (now part of southern Turkey). The Lycians were not Greeks, and from 546 BC they were subject to Persian rule, but they came under the artistic influence of Greece, often employing Greek sculptors on funerary monuments such as this.

6-7 A staircase to the right leads up to the marble **frieze from the Temple of Apollo at Bassae** in Room 6. Room 7 contains a real *coup de théâtre:* the reconstructed

Drinking cup from Camirus, Rhodes, showing Aphrodite riding a goose. Attributed to the Pistoxenos Painter, *c*.460 BC.

Bronze helmet from Corinth, *c*.500 BC.

Amphora showing Achilles killing Penthesilea. Athens *c*.540-530 BC; attributed to the painter Exekias.

Horsemen from the north frieze of the Parthenon, Athens, built 447-438 BC.

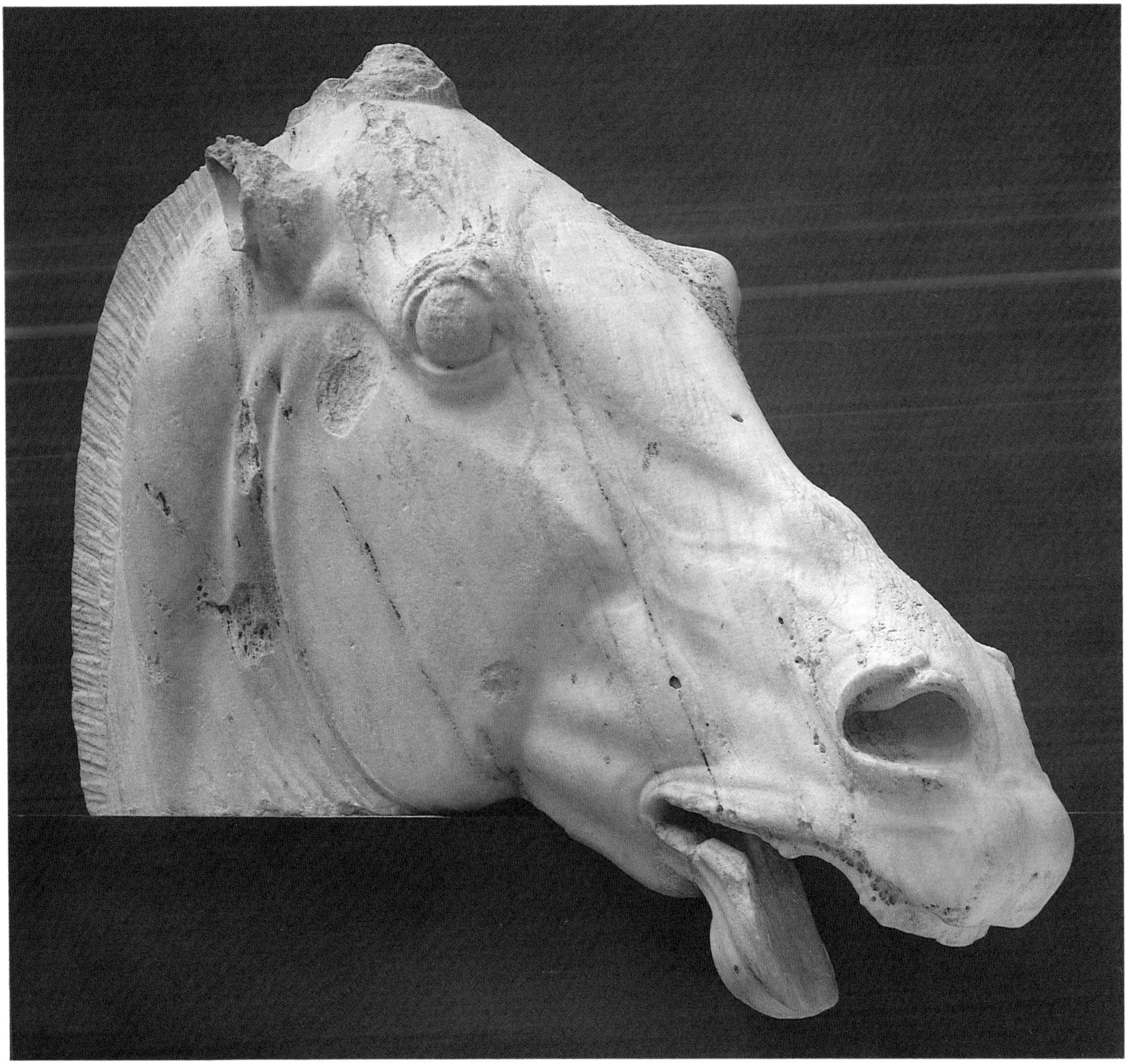

Head of a horse of Selene from the east pediment of the Parthenon.

The Nereid Monument from Xanthos, *c*.400 BC.

brought to London by the Earl of Elgin between 1801 and 1806. (You can hire an excellent recorded commentary at the entrance to the gallery.)

9 Return to the Nereid Room and leave it by the doorway behind the tomb façade to reach Room 9. This room contains more sculptures from the Acropolis at Athens, the most important of which is the tall female **caryatid** on the left – one of the six from the portico of the Erechtheion. The drapery over her right leg hangs so straight as to appear like fluting: indeed, she seems almost in danger of turning into a column herself.

10 Room 10, despite its fine collection of vases, is dominated by another **tomb from Xanthos,** but even this cannot quite overshadow the magnificent **bronze head of a North African** at the end of the room. It comes from Cyrene, and dates from about 350 BC.

12 The highlights of Room 12, to the right of Room 10, are sculptures from two of the Seven Wonders of the World. The **Mausoleum at Halicarnassus** (now Bodrum, on the south-west coast of

Ionic façade of the pedimented tomb of one of the rulers of Xanthos. It is known as the **Nereid Monument,** because the ravishing figures between the columns were once thought to be Nereids. They are now believed to represent sea breezes, but it hardly matters: the important thing about them is their beauty and lightness, and the way their bodies show through their clinging draperies – damp, we may imagine, from the salt sea spray.

8 Half-way along the Nereid Room make a sharp left turn into the Duveen Gallery. On the far side of the glass doors you come face to face with what are probably the most famous of all the treasures of the Museum: the 5th-century BC **sculptures from the Parthenon** in Athens, the most important part of the so-called Elgin Marbles

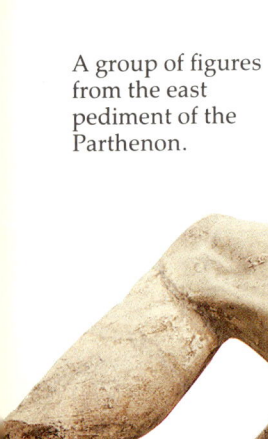

A group of figures from the east pediment of the Parthenon.

Turkey) was the tomb of King Mausolos of Caria, who died shortly before 350 BC. It was a vast columned building set on a high plinth and crowned by a four-horse chariot, and was of such splendour that its fame spread across the whole world of antiquity and gave the word 'mausoleum' to most of the languages of Europe. Alas, the tomb has long since disappeared, but the Museum possesses the head and forequarters of a **horse** from the chariot (with the original bronze bit still clamped between its jaws), together with two statues that used to be thought to represent **Mausolos and his wife** (who was also his sister), Artemisia, although archaeologists now agree that this identification is wrong. The woman's face is sadly damaged, but the man's remains largely intact: it is clearly a portrait from the life, of a man who looks every inch a king even if he wasn't one.

Another Wonder of the World was the **Temple of Artemis at Ephesus.** Its predecessor was destroyed – burnt down deliberately in 356 BC by one Herostratus, for the sole purpose of ensuring that his name should thereby live for ever. (The local authorities made doubly sure that it should do so by passing a decree consigning it to eternal oblivion.) But a new temple was begun at once,

and the huge and magnificent **sculptured drum** from one of 36 similarly carved columns suggests just how spectacular it must have been.

13 With Room 13 we enter the Hellenistic age – the period beginning in 323 BC when, as a result of the conquests of Alexander the Great, Greek culture was carried far beyond the Mediterranean world, through Asia Minor and the Middle East as far as what is now Afghanistan. Here is the celebrated **Demeter of Cnidos,** a majestic figure on her throne; a fine 4th-century bronze head of **Sophocles;** and a really superb bronze head of another goddess, probably **Aphrodite,** dating from about 100 BC. In one of the cases on the right of the room are two particularly charming pieces: a painted group of **two ladies chatting,** and – gently reminiscent of the Aphrodite drinking cup in Room 5 – a figure of **Eros riding a duck.**

Room 14 continues the story of the Hellenistic world into the Roman period. The **winged head of Hypnos** (Sleep), the opulent **marble statue of Apollo** from Cyrene displayed nearby, and the sculptures exhibited at the foot of the steps in Room 15 illustrate the taste of Roman connoisseurs for versions in bronze and marble of Classical and Hellenistic Greek works of art.

For Rome itself you will need to go upstairs to Room 70. The **Portland Vase,** and the **Blacas Cameo,** two masterpieces of early imperial art, are among a wealth of antiquities illustrating Rome and her Empire. A **suit of parade armour sewn from a crocodile's skin** was worn by a Roman soldier stationed in Egypt in the third or fourth century AD. An almost complete silver dinner-service from Chaourse (France) suggests the vulnerability of the frontier in the later Empire. The silver was hidden by worried owners under threat of barbarian invasion in the AD 260s.

From Room 15 you can go down the stairs to the basement, turn left at the bottom and then left again and you will find the Wolfson Galleries, containing several more rooms of Greek and Roman sculptures. These include (in Room 84) the remarkable collection amassed by the 18th-century dilettante Charles Townley. In Room 83 is the largest **marble foot** you have ever seen, part of a colossal statue of Zeus set up in the city of Alexandria.

A pair of marble greyhounds, found with many other figures of dogs at Monte Cagnolo (Dog Mountain), near Rome. Roman, second century AD. Townley Collection (Room 84).

Right. The Blacas Cameo of Augustus, probably made after the emperor's death in AD 14. Carved in sardonyx, the cameo shows Augustus armed with a spear and wearing the protective aegis of the goddess Minerva. It is now displayed in Room 70, case 8.

Left. A winged head of Hypnos (Sleep). A Roman copy in bronze of a lost Greek original, probably of the fourth century BC.

Below. The Portland Vase, made of blue and white glass carved in the cameo technique with mythological scenes. Probably made in Italy around the turn of the first centuries BC and AD. Smashed by a deranged visitor to the Museum in 1845, the vase was restored from more than 200 pieces, and was again restored in 1988-9. It is now displayed in Room 70, case 12.

2. The Western World

The first section of this second part of our tour covers the immensely long period – measurable only in millennia – extending from earliest human times to the 5th century AD when Britain ceased to be a province of the Roman Empire.

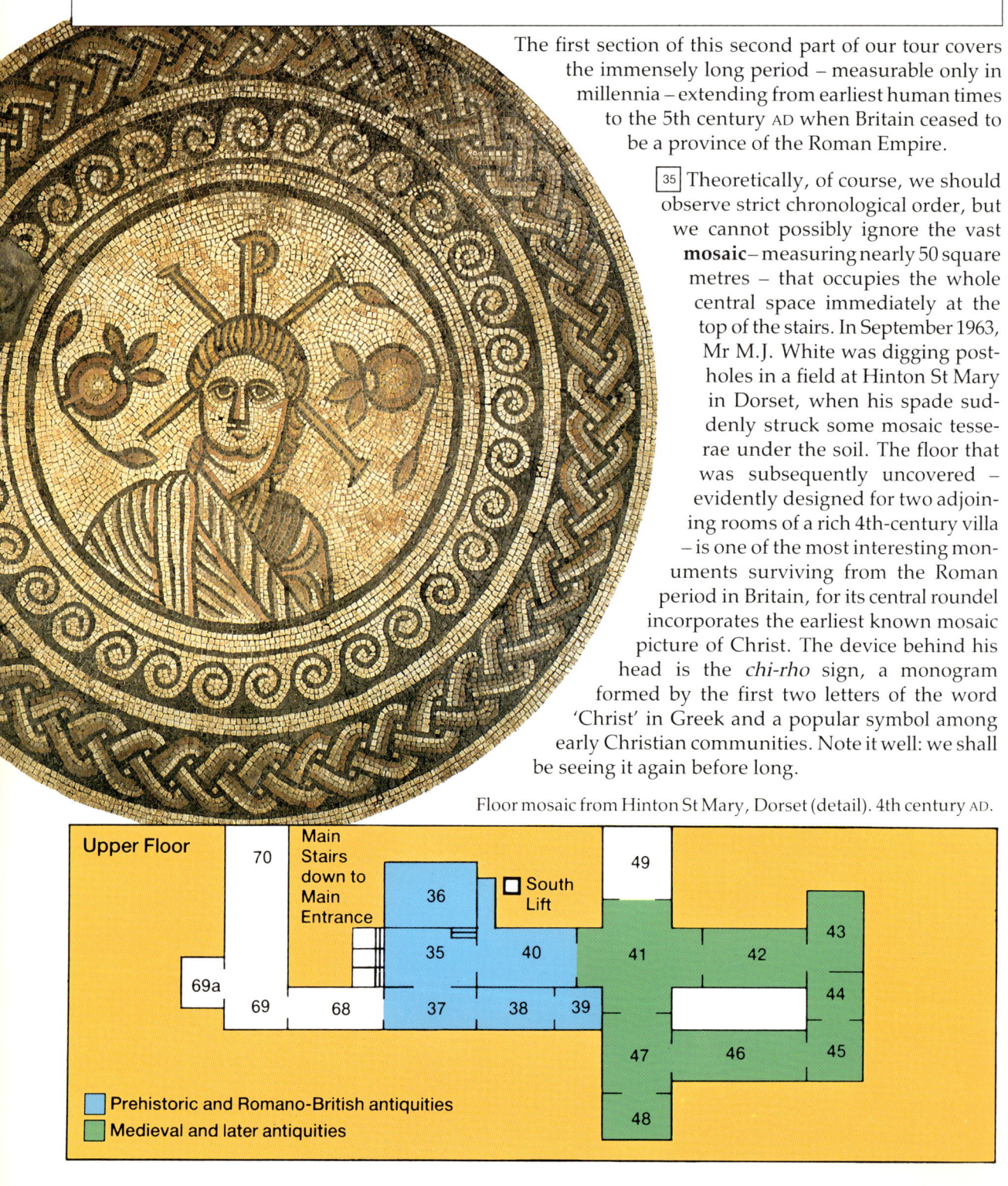

[35] Theoretically, of course, we should observe strict chronological order, but we cannot possibly ignore the vast **mosaic** – measuring nearly 50 square metres – that occupies the whole central space immediately at the top of the stairs. In September 1963, Mr M.J. White was digging post-holes in a field at Hinton St Mary in Dorset, when his spade suddenly struck some mosaic tesserae under the soil. The floor that was subsequently uncovered – evidently designed for two adjoining rooms of a rich 4th-century villa – is one of the most interesting monuments surviving from the Roman period in Britain, for its central roundel incorporates the earliest known mosaic picture of Christ. The device behind his head is the *chi-rho* sign, a monogram formed by the first two letters of the word 'Christ' in Greek and a popular symbol among early Christian communities. Note it well: we shall be seeing it again before long.

Floor mosaic from Hinton St Mary, Dorset (detail). 4th century AD.

Upper Floor

70 | Main Stairs down to Main Entrance

36

☐ South Lift

49

35 | 40 | 41 | 42 | 43

69a

69 | 68 | 37 | 38 | 39

44

47 | 46 | 45

48

■ Prehistoric and Romano-British antiquities
■ Medieval and later antiquities

Prehistoric Europe

36 Now back to prehistory. A short flight of stairs on the left leads up to a gallery devoted to 'man before metals', where you will find a display of artefacts made by our earliest human ancestors. In one of the cases you will see a section of the **Sweet Track,** a raised pathway constructed of wooden planks and stakes, laid across a Somerset marsh nearly 6,000 years ago. In another case are the enigmatic **Folkton Drums,** which were discovered beside the skeleton of a five-year-old child in a tomb of the early Bronze Age in the East Riding of Yorkshire.

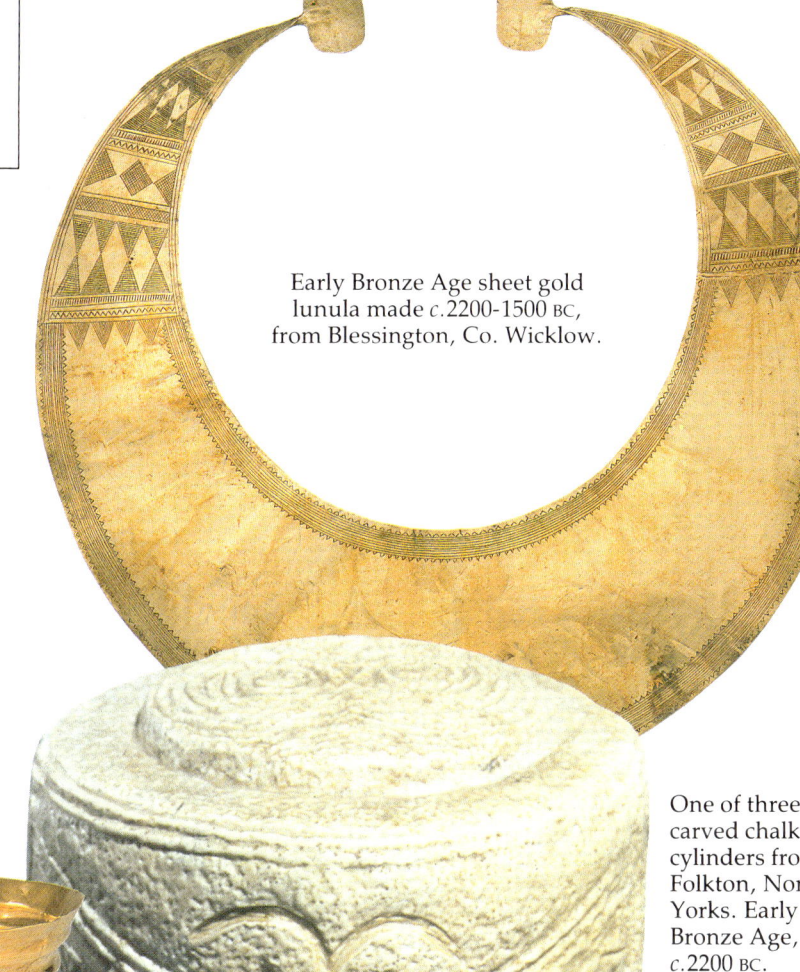

Early Bronze Age sheet gold lunula made *c.*2200-1500 BC, from Blessington, Co. Wicklow.

One of three carved chalk cylinders from Folkton, North Yorks. Early Bronze Age, *c.*2200 BC.

Beaten-gold cup from Rillaton, Cornwall. Early Bronze Age, *c.*1600-1500 BC.

They are solid cylindrical pieces of magnesian limestone carved with curious designs, two of which strongly suggest human faces. What purpose they served remains a mystery.

37 Return down the steps to Room 37, where in one of the cases you will see a little **gold cup** some 8 cm high. It was found in a Bronze Age burial mound at Rillaton in Cornwall in 1837. Beaten from a single ingot in around 1500 BC, it is one of only three such cups ever to have been found in temperate Europe. The burial mound was on land belonging to the Duchy of Cornwall, and the finds, being treasure trove, were therefore sent to King William IV. The cup then disappeared, only to be rediscovered after the death of George V. It was found on the king's dressing table, where it had served as a receptacle for His late Majesty's collar studs.

17

The Celts

Nearby you will see the remains of **Lindow Man.** He was found in a peat-bog in Cheshire in 1984, and probably dates from the Iron Age (*c*.300 BC). His body was unfortunately sliced in half by a peat-cutting machine, but what remains has been thoroughly investigated by medical and forensic scientists. Lindow Man appears to have been the victim of a ritual killing: he was first stunned by a blow to the head, then garrotted with a twisted cord, and finally had his throat cut.

38 Room 38 covers Bronze Age Britain and the early Iron Age in Europe, much of which was occupied at that time by the Celtic peoples. Here we shall find the famous pair of elegant bronze **wine flagons** from Basse-Yutz in Lorraine (France) – truly outstanding examples of early Celtic art. The handles are in the shape of fierce dogs resting their forepaws on the rims, and a tiny duck paddles happily in the stream of wine as it emerges from the spout. The white inlays are in fact of coral (its colour now sadly faded by time), a rare luxury in the Gaul of 400 BC. The flagons show evidence of various stylistic influences, including Persian or Scythian and especially Etruscan art, demonstrating how wide was the Celts' contact with the classical world.

Early Iron Age arms and armour
From left to right. Iron sword with a red enamelled handle and a scabbard with a decorated bronze front plate, *c*.200 BC. Found in 1987 at Kirkburn, East Yorks.

Bronze shield-facing found in the Thames at Battersea. 1st century BC.

Bronze horned helmet from the Thames at Waterloo Bridge. 1st century BC.

Bronze shield, *c*.300 BC, found in the Thames at Chertsey, Surrey.

Decorated bronze shield-front from the River Witham, Lincs, made *c*.200-100 BC.

Lindow Man (before conservation).

Bronze mirror
from Desborough,
Northants. Early 1st
century AD.

39 There were
also fine
craftsmen in
Britain at this
time, as can be
seen in Room 39,
which contains
among many other
exquisite objects two
bronze shield fronts of
spectacular beauty (the
backs would have been of
wood or leather, and have
perished). Both date from the
1st or 2nd century BC, and both
were found in rivers: one in the
Thames and the other in the Witham,
near Lincoln. The first of these, known
as the **Battersea Shield,** is decorated
with flowing scrolls, tendrils and red glass
inlays. The more stylised ornament on the
Witham Shield incorporates five studs of coral,
probably imported from the Mediterranean. Both
shields have animal heads hidden among their
decoration.

Shields like these are still being discovered in
the beds of rivers and lakes – most recently in a
gravel pit at Chertsey, Surrey, in 1985 – and it has
been suggested that armour and weapons may have
been thrown into the water as votive offerings to the
gods. A splendid **bronze helmet** in perfect condition
– the only horned Iron Age helmet so far found in
Britain – was dredged up from the Thames near Waterloo
Bridge. Its owner must have been a man of considerable

importance, perhaps a tribal chieftain, and the jutting horns were probably a symbol of his strength and power. It is, however, extremely fragile, so may not have been used in battle but only on ceremonial occasions.

Other examples of superb craftsmanship are the tremendous **golden torcs** of the 1st century BC. The great majority of them come from East Anglia: Queen Boudica of the Iceni almost certainly wore something of this kind. The greatest of them all, found at Snettisham, Norfolk, in 1950, must surely be one of the most magnificent neck ornaments ever made.

In 1908 some workmen digging for ironstone at Desborough, Northamptonshire, came upon something equally exciting from the same period: a **bronze mirror.** One side was polished to provide a reflective surface, and the other was chased with a sophisticated design that was probably worked out with the aid of a pair of compasses.

In the same room is the dramatic reconstruction of a rich **cremation burial,** probably that of an Iron Age chieftain. This was uncovered in Welwyn Garden City, Hertfordshire, in 1965 by workmen digging a gas main. Dating from the end of the 1st century BC, the burial contained pottery and metal vessels, and a unique set of decorated glass game pieces.

Roman Britain

40 Room 40 immediately to your left contains a collection of remarkable objects dating from the Roman administration of Britain, which began with the invasion of AD 43 and continued for some 400 years. You will see that they are quite different from the Roman objects shown downstairs. Those were largely from Rome itself, or at least from Italy, and the emphasis was on stone and marble statuary. What we shall see here tends to be far more intimate and domestic: objects designed to be used rather than simply admired, and made – more often than not – by native British craftsmen. But though the taste and style may on occasion seem less sophisticated, you will still find craftsmanship here to take your breath away.

On the wall at the far end you will see parts of a suite of **wall-**

Torc from Snettisham, Norfolk, made from an alloy of gold, silver and copper in the 1st century BC.

Part of a set of coloured glass gaming-pieces from an Iron Age burial at Welwyn Garden City, Herts, c.10 BC – AD 10.

Praying figure: a Christian wall-painting from Lullingstone Roman villa, Kent. 4th century AD.

Facing page. Detail of the Great Dish from the Mildenhall Treasure, found in Suffolk. Silver, 4th century AD.

paintings from the chapel of a villa at Lullingstone in Kent. These were found reduced to tiny fragments of plaster and have been meticulously reconstructed in the Museum's laboratories. Surviving from the 4th century – the early days of Christianity in these islands – they may be considered as a sort of mural counterpart to the Hinton St Mary floor. In one of the panels you will see the *chi-rho* sign again, this time with two more Greek letters, one on each side: they are *alpha* and *omega,* the first and last in the alphabet, used by Christians to signify that Christ is the beginning and the end.

The *chi-rho* sign turns up again on several pieces of silverware of much the same date from the **Water Newton Treasure,** found near Peterborough in Cambridgeshire and probably the oldest set of church plate from anywhere in the Roman world. What makes these pieces still more interesting is their comparatively plain style and matt finish, two characteristics which, since they are unparalleled elsewhere in the Roman world, suggest that they may in fact have been made in Britain.

In another case you will find a collection of thin slivers of wood. They may not seem very exciting at first glance, but if you look at them carefully you will see line after line of writing in many different hands. These are just a few of the **Vindolanda tablets,** found among the ruins of a Roman fort of that name near Hadrian's Wall in Northumbria. Consisting for the most part of official military documents and letters to members of the garrison at Vindolanda, they are the oldest dated handwritten documents in the country and they give a remarkable insight into the life of a Roman garrison in a remote outpost.

There is much else to catch our attention in this room: some marvellous **Roman glass,** for example, and a desirable set of spoons with stylised ducks' heads, from the **Thetford Treasure.** Including some 38 gold items, this hoard was probably the stock-in-trade of a high-class jeweller or merchant; it was made either in Gaul or in Britain and buried towards the end of the 4th century AD. Perhaps most magnificent of all, however, is the **Mildenhall Treasure,** 28 stunning pieces of 4th-century silver tableware, discovered on the edge of the Suffolk fens during winter ploughing in the early 1940s. The centrepiece – a great dish over 60 cm across and weighing over 8 kg – is a glorious riot of pagan gods and nymphs, satyrs and sea-horses, whirling round in a frenzied Bacchic dance.

The end of Roman rule in Britain, unlike its beginning, was not marked by a single event but by a gradual disintegration of central authority around the end of the 4th century. There was no mass exodus of Romans, rather a long period of adjustment as Romano-British communities reacted to an influx of Saxon and other settlers, whose arrival can be taken as the beginning of the medieval period in Britain.

The Middle Ages

41 Our tour of the medieval galleries begins in Room 41. Its *pièce de résistance,* half-way down the room on the right, is another exciting collection of buried treasure, one of the richest ever discovered in the British Isles: the **Sutton Hoo ship burial.** It was in July 1939 that archaeologists found the remains of a great Anglo-Saxon ship, which had been dragged some 600 yards up a steep slope from the River Deben in Suffolk to serve as the last resting-place of a king. Who he was we do not know for certain, but he must have been a ruler of great wealth and international prestige, because his burial chamber in the ship contained a magnificent collection of objects from all over Europe and as far away as Byzantium. Look for example at the marvellous silver bowls in case 54 and the ceremonial gold jewellery lavishly decorated with garnets and *millefiori* glass in case 56. The splendid helmet is indeed fit for a king, as is the shield with its remarkable elaborate mounts. But the story of Sutton Hoo deserves proper telling, and you will find it admirably told on each side of the doorway into Room 47.

It would be a pity, however, to allow the Sutton Hoo ship burial to blind us to the other treasures of Room 41: the **Franks Casket,** for example, in case 43, carved out of whale's bone in Northumbria in about AD 750 and depicting scenes from classical legend, Germanic mythology and the Bible; or, close to the door into Room 49, the fine 4th-century **sarcophagus** with its carving of Jonah and the whale; or, again, immediately to the left of this, in case 21, the famous **Lycurgus Cup** of the fourth century AD, carved with amazing virtuosity from a single blank (or piece) of glass which, while normally the colour of green pea soup, turns a rich wine-red under transmitted light. And don't miss the sophisticated 9th-century **silver brooches** in case 46 or the outsize Viking ones in case 50. (Even in the 8th century, one feels, these must have seemed a little over the top!) In the same case is part of the **Cuerdale Hoard,** buried by the banks of the River Ribble in Lancashire in about AD 903 and discovered in 1840. Probably loot brought to safety by the Vikings after their expulsion from Dublin, it contained over 7000 coins, to say nothing of silver ingots and hacked-up jewellery – a total of 88 pounds of silver and the largest Viking hoard found outside Russia.

The Sutton Hoo ship burial (after AD 624/5): the excavated ship, looking towards the prow, and some of the objects it contained.

From top. Fragments of an iron helmet originally covered with panels of tinned-bronze sheeting stamped with animal interlace or figures. The nose, mouth, eyebrows and animal-headed crest terminals are of gilded cast bronze, the eyebrows inlaid with silver wire and set with garnets.

Purse lid: gold and cloisonné garnet units mounted on a modern base.

Gold shoulder-clasps decorated with cloisonné garnets and millefiori glass.

Gold belt-buckle decorated with animal interlace.

The Franks casket, made of whale's bone in the 8th century AD and decorated with scenes from the Christian, Germanic and Roman traditions.

Walrus ivory chess-piece (king) found on the Isle of Lewis (*right*). Probably Scandinavian, mid-12th century.

42 The best-loved item in Room 42 is surely the group of walrus **ivory chessmen** in the second case on the left. They were found in a small stone shelter half-hidden beneath a sandbank on the island of Lewis in 1831. Among the 67 pieces on display (the Museum actually possesses 82, and there are 11 more in Edinburgh) are 8 kings and queens, so they must be the remains of at least four complete sets. (They all appear to be white pieces only because the red dye on many of them has been worn or washed away.) The style is Scandinavian, the date probably mid-12th century, but how they found their way to the Outer Hebrides we shall never know.

You should look closely, too, at the superb Byzantine **icons** in the first case on the left. In this country we often tend to forget that – at least until 1204, when it was sacked by the forces of the Fourth Crusade – the city of Constantinople, capital of the Byzantine Empire, was celebrated all over Europe and beyond as the most brilliant, cultivated and sumptuous in the world – a city that had escaped the barbarian invasions which had threatened to extinguish the civilisation of the west and that had kept alive the traditions of antiquity throughout the Dark Ages. Byzantine art, even more than western, was steeped in the Christian religion, though its style was far more hieratic and formalised. Take, for example, the splendid portrait of **St Peter,** almost certainly of the early 14th century, and compare it with the far smaller icon of similar date depicting four **New Testament scenes.** The techniques could hardly be more different: broad sweeping strokes on the one hand and meticulous delicacy on the other. Both, however, seem to radiate that strange spirituality which is inseparable from the art of the Christian east. Loveliest of all, perhaps, is the wooden panel portraying **John the Baptist,** which seems to have been painted in Constantinople around

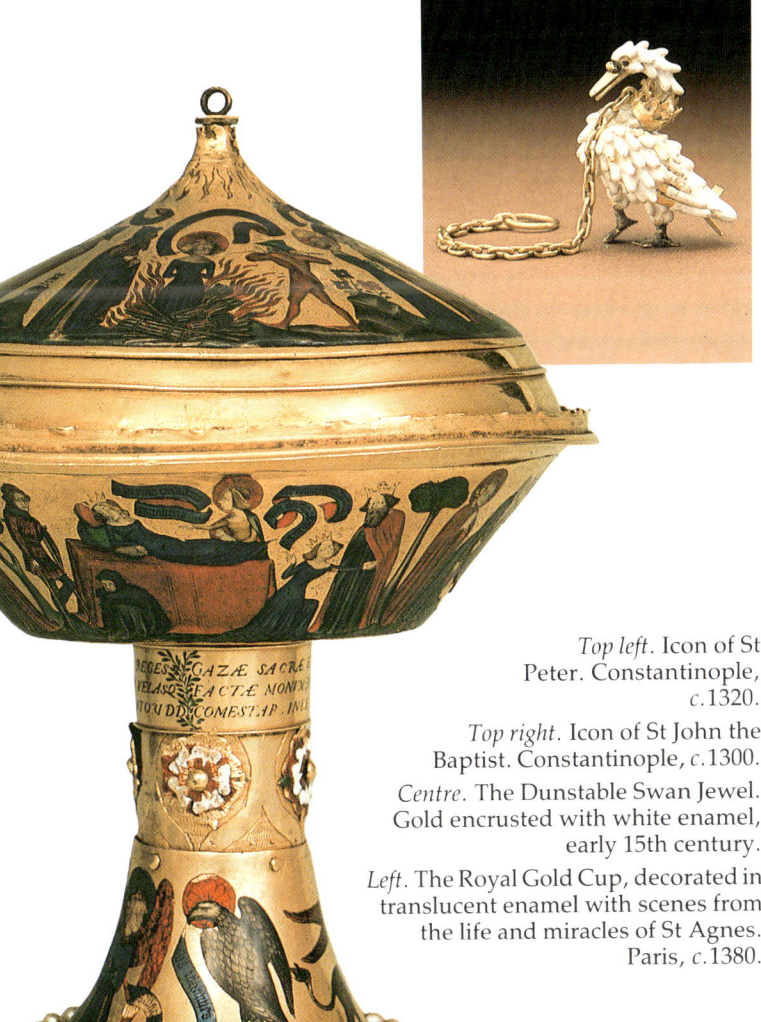

1300. Its exquisite quality suggests that it probably belonged to some great noble or minister of the court, if not to the Emperor himself.

Further down the room, after two magnificent cases devoted to Gothic art, we come to displays of medieval jewellery, secular life, popular religion and arms and armour. The **jewellery** case reveals the ostentatious as well as the tender side of life in the Middle Ages: gold brooches with love inscriptions, and other pieces set with precious stones, some even invested with magical properties to protect the wearer against disease and sudden death. Perhaps the most appealing is the tiny early 15th-century gold and enamel **swan brooch** from Dunstable, a symbol of the House of Lancaster.

One of the finest of all medieval musical instruments is the beautiful boxwood **gittern,** made between 1290 and 1330 and carved with minute hunting scenes amid intricate foliage. Then, at the far end of the room, you must on no account miss the magnificent Flemish **shield of parade** – like the Celtic ones in Room 38, it was obviously never intended for actual use – depicting a knight and his lady. The most opulent object in the entire room, however, is the **'Royal Gold Cup'** in a case nearby. This dazzling piece, the property of the kings first of France and later of England, was made by a Parisian goldsmith in about 1380. Its polychrome enamels depict scenes from the life of St Agnes, while the symbols of the Evangelists encircle the base.

If you like medieval pottery and tiles, you will find plenty to interest you in Room 43; but time is getting short and you may prefer to turn straight to Room 44, immediately to the right of it. Here, somewhat surprisingly, your ears will be assailed even before your eyes are, by a continual chorus of ticking, of humming and whirring, of ringing and chiming: you are entering the Gallery of Clocks and Watches.

Top left. Icon of St Peter. Constantinople, *c.*1320.

Top right. Icon of St John the Baptist. Constantinople, *c.*1300.

Centre. The Dunstable Swan Jewel. Gold encrusted with white enamel, early 15th century.

Left. The Royal Gold Cup, decorated in translucent enamel with scenes from the life and miracles of St Agnes. Paris, *c.*1380.

Clocks and Watches

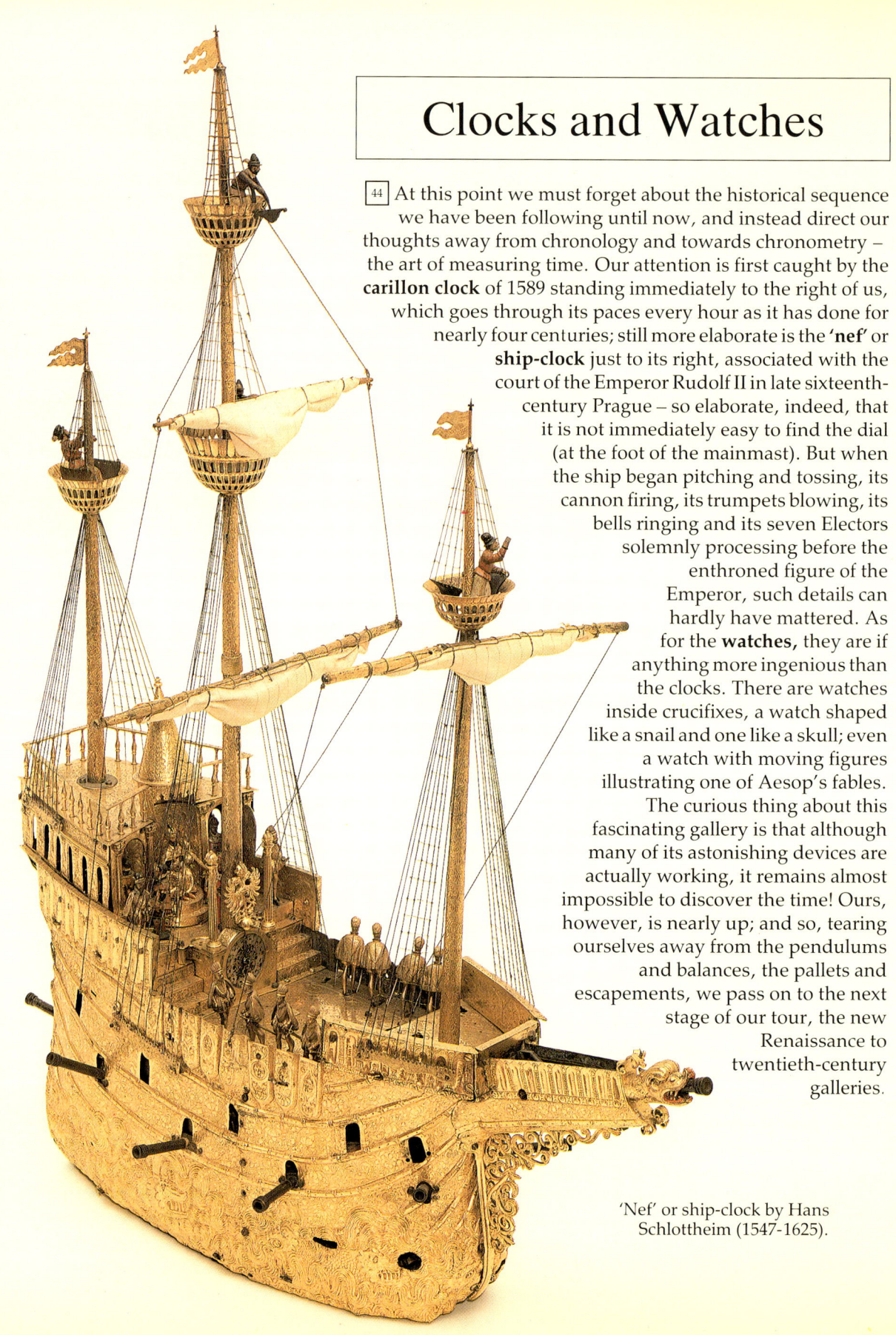

[44] At this point we must forget about the historical sequence we have been following until now, and instead direct our thoughts away from chronology and towards chronometry – the art of measuring time. Our attention is first caught by the **carillon clock** of 1589 standing immediately to the right of us, which goes through its paces every hour as it has done for nearly four centuries; still more elaborate is the **'nef'** or **ship-clock** just to its right, associated with the court of the Emperor Rudolf II in late sixteenth-century Prague – so elaborate, indeed, that it is not immediately easy to find the dial (at the foot of the mainmast). But when the ship began pitching and tossing, its cannon firing, its trumpets blowing, its bells ringing and its seven Electors solemnly processing before the enthroned figure of the Emperor, such details can hardly have mattered. As for the **watches,** they are if anything more ingenious than the clocks. There are watches inside crucifixes, a watch shaped like a snail and one like a skull; even a watch with moving figures illustrating one of Aesop's fables. The curious thing about this fascinating gallery is that although many of its astonishing devices are actually working, it remains almost impossible to discover the time! Ours, however, is nearly up; and so, tearing ourselves away from the pendulums and balances, the pallets and escapements, we pass on to the next stage of our tour, the new Renaissance to twentieth-century galleries.

'Nef' or ship-clock by Hans Schlottheim (1547-1625).

Renaissance to Twentieth Century

Boxwood miniature altarpiece carved with scenes from the Life and Passion of Christ. Flemish, early 16th century.

45 To enter Room 45 is to find yourself in an Aladdin's cave. Every other room we have visited has contained pieces from a number of different owners; here we come to **The Waddesdon Bequest**, a single group of very diverse items, all amassed by one man and bequeathed to the Museum on condition that they were kept together in one room. That man was Baron Ferdinand Rothschild MP, and the treasures here constitute only a fraction of his complete collection. (The rest of it can still be seen at Waddesdon in Buckinghamshire, now the property of the National Trust.)

It is an almost impossible task to select outstanding items from a collection such as this, but perhaps two of the most memorable are the tiny Flemish **boxwood altarpiece,** carved in 1511 with the utmost delicacy, and the gold enamelled **reliquary** made in Paris at the command of the Duc de Berry in the first years of the fifteenth century for the preservation of one of the thorns from Christ's crown.

46 The next two galleries have recently been refurbished and many of the original architectural features restored. With Room 46, **Europe, 15th-18th centuries,** we continue the sequence of European history from the Renaissance to the French Revolution. Among the highlights of artistic production from *c.*1450 to the end of the 18th century you will find Venetian glass, painted ceramics of the Italian Renaissance and Hispano-Moresque pottery, Elizabethan silver (including the recently-acquired 'Armada Service'), porcelain from Meissen, Sèvres, Chelsea, and other celebrated factories. The central section looks at trade with the Far East and with South America and, perhaps the most fascinating, the extraordinary range of exotic items brought back to Europe from distant lands.

47 Room 47 is **Europe, the 19th century. The T. Y. Chao Gallery**. From the influence of the classical world (make sure you see Josiah Wedgwood's celebrated copy of the Portland vase), we move through the Romantic Movement and the Gothic Revival to the pioneering work of Christopher Dresser and the eclecticism of the late-19th century. The gallery is dominated by the remarkable Hull Grundy Gift of jewellery, containing pieces designed by Castellani, Giuliano, Boucheron, Tiffany and many others.

48 If you are interested in the **20th century,** turn left into Room 48, which contains changing displays of European and American decorative arts from 1900 to *c.*1950. Here you will find continental Art Nouveau, Russian Revolutionary porcelain, ceramics and metalwork from the Bauhaus in Germany and a range of recent acquisitions, for this is an area where the Museum is constantly adding to its collections. Next time you visit, there is bound to be something new.

French fin-de-siècle brooch in gold, coral, pearl, diamonds and a ruby. The female head is a personification of France with a cap of Liberty. Designed by René Bouvet, Paris, *c.* 1900. Hull Grundy Gift.

3. The Oriental World

Entering the Museum from the North, or walking through from the south, you reach the magnificent Asian collections, beginning with the Islamic gallery on the ground floor.

John Addis Islamic Gallery

On display here are objects from the Museum's extensive Islamic collection ranging from Moorish Spain to Mughal India and from the 7th century to the present day. The gallery follows a broadly geographical and chronological sequence with additional thematic

Sultan Husayn in 1712 and so Sloane must have acquired it within years of its manufacture.

The glass collection bequeathed to the Museum by Felix Slade included a number of gilt and enamelled mosque lamps and vessels dating from 13th and 14th century Egypt and Syria. One of these is the unique pilgrim bottle painted with arabesque and animated scrollwork on the front and back and depictions of horsemen and musicians on the shoulders in richly coloured enamels (case 21).

The Blacas ewer is an exceptionally fine example of medieval inlaid brass (case 12). It was made in Mosul in northern Iraq in 1232 by Shuja' b. Man'a, one of the best inlayers in the city, and is covered with scenes of contemporary courtlife.

displays for coinage (case 44), science and magic (case 45) and arms and armour (case 46). A special area in the centre is dedicated to the temporary exhibition of a selection of miniature paintings and other works too delicate for permanent display.

Among the greatest treasures in this gallery is a magnificent brass astrolabe which has been in the Museum since its foundation by Sir Hans Sloane in 1753 (case 2). It was made in Isfahan for the Safavid Shah

Large blue and white ceramic bowl, Iznik, 16th century

A large number of lustre and Iznik pottery vessels came from the collection of Frederick DuCane Godman, a 19th century ornithologist. A tall albarello decorated with courtly figures and bold arabesques demonstrates why the lustre technique was so highly esteemed after its discovery by Arab potters in the 9th century (case 16). This vessel, used for the storage of dry foodstuffs, was made in Kashan in Iran in the late 12th century.

The Museum's collection of Iznik pottery from Ottoman Turkey is unsurpassed thanks to Godman and his contemporary, the antiquarian John Henderson. Two large bowls made at Iznik in the 16th century (case 32) are decorated with exotic blossoms and leaves and can be compared directly to the finest court textiles of the Ottoman period.

One of the most extraordinary objects in the gallery is the large jade terrapin (case 43) found at the bottom of a tank in Allahabad, which was probably made for the Mughal Emperor Akbar or his son Jahangir. This life-sized reptile is carved from a single piece of Siberian jade with great skill and naturalism and is the centrepiece of a display of decorative arts from Mughal India (case 42).

Joseph E. Hotung Gallery

This extends the whole length of the North side of the Museum on the first floor, where you will find the major collections from China, the Indian Subcontinent and Southeast Asia. This gallery can also be reached from the South side of the Museum via the east stairs at the end of the King's Library and the Oriental Corridor (room 33b) where you will see temporary displays of oriental prints and drawings. Begin your tour of the Hotung gallery by the well in its centre.

Turning to your right you will see an introductory panel to the Chinese collections showing two items typically associated with China, a bronze ritual vessel and a blue and white flask.

Portrait of a Confucian scholar. 18th century.

Korea

The arts of Korea, principally from the Koryo and Choson dynasties, are at present displayed on the North staircase and in the North Entrance where in addition a few pieces of contemporary Korean ceramics are also shown. These are a part of an expanding collection of contemporary Korean paintings, prints, ceramics and decorative arts. A new gallery for Korean art will open after the removal of the British Library.

Bronze ram *zun*, Shang dynasty, 12-11th century BC.

Porcelain flask with underglaze blue decoration. 1426-35 period of the Ming dynasty.

From there you will begin with Chinese Neolithic culture of the period *c.* 5000-2000 BC showing pottery and ritual jade pieces. Bronzes and jades were more highly esteemed by the Chinese than the gold and silver preferred in the West. These circular and tubular jades, *bi* and *cong* and axes were obviously very important to the Chinese in the ceremonials surrounding life and death and have been found buried in large numbers.

The bronze age in China is represented by many ritual vessels, bells, weapons and chariot fittings dating from *c.* 2000-250 BC. In case 3 you can see the step-by-step process in the manufacture of Chinese bronze casting, which they practised from very early days on a large scale. Look at case 6 where we have displayed bronzes with inscriptions, which are very important historical documents. The *Kang Hou gui* ritual food vessel, for example, records that the king gave territory as a reward to his brother the duke of Kang on the occasion of an attack on the king's enemies (*c.* 1050 BC).

From here we jump several centuries to the Han dynasty (206 BC - AD 220) where in case 14 you will see various lacquered items. Among these is a cup, dated to AD 4, which has an inscription recording the number and names of the craftsmen who were involved in its manufacture and the government personnel who supervised it. This underlines the mass-production methods already seen in bronze manufacture and which were applied to other materials such as lacquer and ceramics. To the side, in case 17, are various models which the Han people took with them to their graves, to be used in the afterlife, such as fish ponds, sheep pens, and games such as *liu bo* which you can see two people playing in the bottom left hand corner.

The Tang dynasty of China (AD 618-906) was one of the most resplendent periods of Chinese history. In the showcase in the centre of the gallery, case 47, stand the magnificent tomb figurines buried with General Liu Tingxun who died in 728. There are Buddhist guardian figures to protect him in the afterlife, civil and military officials to represent him, horses and grooms and the camels which travelled along the desert routes of the Silk Road.

In case 24 you can see Chinese silver of the Tang dynasty. Then look across at the ceramics in case 27 which shows some of China's earliest porcelain, made well over a thousand years before Europe learned how to make it. Looking at these two cases shows you the close interaction in shapes and form between the two materials. The Song dynasty (960-1279) is considered by the Chinese to have been one of their most refined artistic periods and its very fine porcelain they judge to be the most perfect ever made. Look at the very finely made Yue and *ding* wares in cases 27 and 28; and on the other side (case 29) the very rare Ru ware, a blueish-green ware probably trying to imitate jade, and only manufactured for about twenty years for the imperial court of the Northern Song period (960-1126). Also look at the celadon and *qingbai* in case 31.

The eastern end of the gallery is dominated by the large Ming dynasty (1368-1644) Buddhist fresco of three Bodhisattvas, and this is flanked by Buddhist figures in different materials and from different periods, designed to give an impression of how such figures were displayed in Chinese temples.

Cases 35, 36 and 37 show the development of the Chinese script, from its earliest appearance on oracle bones to a page from a modern Chinese dictionary showing the script of today. Items used by the scholar are also displayed such as brushes, inkcakes, inkstones and waterdroppers.

Blue and white porcelain is what most people think of in association with China and the gallery has a very fine display of both underglaze blue and underglaze red decorated porcelain dating

Luohan ceramic figure, Liao dynasty, 907-1124.

from its early days in the Yuan dynasty (1279-1368) when it was principally made for the Middle Eastern market (see the dishes in case 38) and its maturity in the Ming (1368-1644) dynasty when it was made in Chinese taste and for imperial use (case 41). As a contrast, look at the very fine, white stemcup from the Ming dynasty, (top shelf case 40) with its discreet dragon incised between the glazes. You can only see this if you stand back and catch it in the light.

The following cases contain examples of decorative art including cloisonée and lacquer. Chinese artisans were for the most part anonymous craftsmen but in case 43, middle shelf away from the window, we have a carved lacquered plate dating to 1489, the Pingliang plate, where the maker has signed his name as well as the date. In case 53 you can now see copied in porcelain the ritual items originally made in bronze (case 6), illustrating the Chinese practice of copying old forms. On the Chinese-style stepped shelving are displayed many items which would have been collected by the Chinese themselves during the Qing dynasty (1644-1911). These cases also reveal the technical virtuosity of the Qing dynasty craftsmen who could make porcelain to look like bronze or glass (no. 17 in case 58) and glass to look like realgar (no. 5 in case 59).

In case 61 you will see Chinese porcelain made for the West to order, often from drawings sent from Europe. Look at the Crucifixion plates on the left and in the central case, top shelf, Chinese porcelain painted by the Chinese with Western figures and below a cup and saucer made in China but painted in the West, in Bohemia about 1720-30, with the Chinoiserie figures then fashionable.

The South and Southeast Asian, and Chinese sections meet in the middle of the gallery. Buddhism and trade were the two main links

Goddess Tara, Sri Lanka, 8th century AD.

which joined these large and influential areas of the world and in these final cases in the Chinese section of the gallery are displayed items found on the Silk Route along which Buddhism and trade travelled into China.

South and Southeast Asia

Back at the well of the gallery, if you now turn left and head westwards, you will see a magnificent bronze sculpture of *Shiva* of *c.* 950 AD. This powerful figure was cast by the lost wax method and reflects the intense emotion characteristic of the devotees of *Shiva* in the South India of the Chola kings (*c.* mid 9th to 13th century AD). The other sculpture is a Javanese guardian figure representing the Southeastern Asian parts of the collection. The intention in this half of the gallery is to emphasise the role of images or fragments of architecture as functioning parts of sacred buildings and as objects of worship, not only as works of art.

Just beyond the well is one of the masterpieces of this collection, the nearly lifesize figure of the goddess Tara, dating to the 8th century AD. Further on are two serene sandstone sculptures of the Buddha from Sarnath, in north India, of the 5th-6th century AD.

The bronze image of the Hindu god *Shiva* as 'Lord of the Dance' (Nataraja), dating to about AD 1100, dominates the middle of the gallery (case 37). The four arms of the image hold symbols which characterise the deity.

Returning to the theme of Buddhism, note in case 18, top shelf, the Bimaran reliquary, a small gold cylindrical vessel studded with garnets and bearing two standing images of the Buddha and various deities. This rare object dates from the lst century AD and is important because the images on it are amongst the earliest surviving representations of the Buddha in human form.

Between cases 22 and 24, you will find a small Central Indian shrine dating to the 17th-18th century which displays the essential parts of a north Indian Hindu temple. The tower structure suggests the Himalayas, mountain home of the gods.

In the centre of the gallery is a large black stone sculpture from Orissa on the east coast of India. Dating from the 12th century AD, it depicts the Hindu god *Shiva* and his consort *Parvati* seated in amorous embrace, their divinity indicated by their many arms and their great size relative to the surrounding figures, many of whom play instruments. At the base, their son, elephant-headed *Ganesha*, is shown. Close to him are the animals associated with *Shiva* (bull) and *Parvati* (lion).

Bronze image of the Hindu deity *Shiva Nataraja*, c. 1100 AD.

Bronze sculpture of the Buddha, Burma, 12-13th century AD, Pagan Period.

Bimaran reliquary, Gandhara, 1st-3rd century AD.

Asahi Shimbun Gallery of Amaravati Sculpture

Drum slab from the Amaravati stupa. 3rd century AD.

At the west end of the gallery is an architectural display of the magnificent sculptured slabs from the 2nd-3rd century AD Buddhist stupa at Amaravati in southeast India. A section of the railing which surrounded the stupa is held on a metal frame in front of part of the foundation platform, and sculptures from the dome of the original structure are mounted on the back wall. The narrative reliefs on the inside of the railing depict events in the life of the Buddha. In the earliest slabs the Buddha is shown in symbolic form – an empty throne or sets of footprints - but by the third century he was depicted in human form. Sculptures from the drum of the stupa illustrate how it appeared in the 3rd century AD.

As you leave the Asahi Shimbun gallery you will see on the north and south sides cases devoted to regions of South Asia, Southeast Asia and the Himalayan regions.

Leaving the Hotung gallery note the great 6th-century marble figure of the Buddha *Amitabha* in the stairwell.

Woodblock print by Shiko Munakata, 1964

Japan

92-94 The Japanese collections are probably the most comprehensive in their scope in Europe. They cover all aspects of material culture from the Jomon period (beginning *c.* 10,000 BC) until the present day and are particularly rich in ceramics, laquerware, sculpture, painting and prints. The important holdings of Ukiyoe prints have been complemented in recent years by the continuing collection of modern prints, one of which is shown on the left.

The Japanese Gallery which opened in 1990 was built in the roofspace at the top of the King Edward VII building, generously supported by many organisations and individuals in Japan and the UK. It houses changing displays of the Museum's own material, and loan exhibitions from Japan. A permanent feature of the gallery is the Tea House donated by the Urasenke Foundation of Kyoto, in which the tea ceremony is occasionally performed.

Prints and Drawings

Left. Albrecht Dürer (1471-1528): *Study of water, sky and pine trees*. Watercolour and body colour.

Right. William Blake (1757-1826), *The Ancient of Days*, from *Europe, a prophecy*, 1794. Relief etching and watercolour.

The Department houses one of the most representative and distinguished collections of Western prints and drawings in existence. Geographically the scope of the collection covers Europe and those societies culturally associated with it in other parts of the world, principally the United States, Canada, Latin America, Australia, New Zealand and Israel. It contains approximately three million works on paper from the fifteenth century to the present day, covering the entire history of the major graphic arts as well as including important collections of ephemera.

The greatest strengths of the collection lie in the fields of Old Master prints and drawings from all schools, satires of the eighteenth centuries, and British material of all periods. Since the mid-1970s particular attention has been given to improving the representation of work executed from the late nineteenth century to the present day.

With the exception of Michelangelo's cartoon, 'Epifania', and Dürer's print 'The Triumphal Arch of Emperor Maximilian', the collections are not on permanent display because of their fragility and susceptibility to light; however, temporary exhibitions can be seen throughout the year. For admission to the Students' Room please apply to the Department.

Sandro Botticelli, *Abundance*, *c*.1478. Pen and ink and wash over black chalk.

Odilon Redon (1840-1916), *La Cellule d'or*, 1893. Oil and gold metallic paint.

Rembrandt van Rijn (1606-69): *Girl sleeping*. Brush drawing in brown ink.

Ernst Ludwig Kirchner (1880-1938), *Portrait of Otto Müller*, 1915. Colour woodcut.

Coins and Medals

The Department of Coins and Medals houses one of the world's finest numismatic collections, containing over 600,000 coins, medals, banknotes, tokens and badges. Most of these are stored in the department, available for study by researchers. A gallery devoted to the history of money is planned, and Room 69a shows temporary exhibitions from the department's holdings, changing several times a year. Furthermore, many coins are on display throughout the museum, exhibited in the context of the cultures which produced them. Some serve to document the history of coinage, while others illustrate

Silver decadrachm of Syracuse, Sicily, signed by the engraver Kimon, 4th century BC.

aspects of history, art and daily life.

Coinage began in Asia Minor in the 7th century BC and case 3 in the Archaic Greece Gallery (Room 3) illustrates this crucial development. Upstairs Greek and Roman coinage is well represented in galleries 69 to 73, showing how vital coins are to our understanding of the ancient world. In Room 69 coins are used to illustrate themes such as Everyday Life and Gods and Heroes. Some are works of art in their own right, for instance the decadrachms of Syracuse and

Copper coin of Hosam al-Din Arslan, ruler of the Artuqids of Mardin (modern south-east Turkey and northern Syria), struck in 1199 (AH 596). The figure derives from the astrological symbol for the planet Mars.

Acragas, their superb designs signed by the engravers taking pride in their skill (Room 73, case 69).

The impact of Greek and Roman civilisation encouraged the spread of coinage to the Celts of Europe (Room 39, case 11). From its origins in Asia Minor the use of coinage also spread to the western Asiatic empires of the Achaemenids, the Parthians and the Sassanians (Rooms 51 and 52). The Oxus Treasure reveals the coinage in use on the eve of Alexander the Great's conquests (Room 51, case 14). Coinage of the Islamic world is displayed in cases 44 and 45 in the John Addis Islamic Gallery (Room 35).

Coinage had developed independently in China in the 7th century BC, as is shown in the Hotung Gallery (cases 21 and 55).

Coins in Rooms 41 and 42 illustrate their importance as evidence for the history of medieval Europe. Coinage is also integrated into Rooms 46 and 47, where it is joined by the medal, an art form developed in 15th-century Italy to commemorate personalities and events, often making it the ideal medium to indicate the historical context of these galleries.

Bronze medal of the Byzantine emperor John VIII Palaeologus, by Antonio Pisanello, 1438.

Ethnography

The Museum of Mankind in Burlington Gardens near Piccadilly is the showcase for the British Museum's ethnography collections, from an enormous range of the world's cultures. These represent the indigenous peoples of the whole of the Americas, Australia and the Pacific Islands, most of Africa, large areas of Asia and parts of Europe. This is the place to learn about the cultural traditions of smaller-scale societies of the present or recent times as well as certain cultures which are known mainly through archaeology.

Only a selection of the large collections can be exhibited at one time, and this is done mainly through temporary exhibitions which look into particular traditions which deserve to be better known in the Western world. Among the exhibitions of 1994 is 'Paradise', which shows how a people of the Papua New Guinea Highlands have adapted the products and culture of the wider world to develop their own cultural traditions in new ways. An exhibition on Benin includes some of the remarkable brass and ivory sculptures for which this Nigerian kingdom is so famous, and a very different African society is illustrated by the beautiful woodcarvings and raffia cloth from the Kuba people of Zaire. There is a new gallery devoted to changing exhibitions of the textiles which form such an important part of the ethnography collections. A selection of famous works of art from around the world is also constantly on display.

A new permanent exhibition will also be opening soon at the main British Museum, to represent the ancient civilisations of Mexico. In future years more new exhibitions will open there as the Ethnography Department is reunited with the rest of the British Museum after more than twenty years at the Museum of Mankind.

Benin brass sculpture

Wahgi painted shield

Northwest Coast sculpture

The British Museum

Great Russell Street
London WC1B3DG
Tel. 071-636 1555
Recorded Information 071-580 1788

OPENING HOURS Monday to Saturday 10-5, Sunday 2.30-6. Closed during the Christmas period, New Year's day, Good Friday and the first Monday in May. Every effort is made to keep the galleries open during these hours, but essential work may necessitate closing certain areas without notice. Clearance of the galleries begins approximately ten minutes before closing time. Smoking, eating and drinking are not allowed in the Museum.

REFRESHMENTS The Museum Café offers a variety of snacks and beverages, and the licensed Restaurant a choice of full meals in comfortable and relaxed surroundings.

INFORMATION The Information Desk is located in the Front Hall of the Museum.

GUIDED TOURS Tickets for tours of the highlights of the Museum may be purchased in the Front Hall.

EDUCATION The Events programme of lectures, gallery talks and films, covering a two-monthly period, is available from the Information Desk or by joining the mailing list (annual subscription). The offices of the Museum Education Service are at 38 Russell Square. The Education Service can advise teachers, and offers talks and study days for students, teachers and other interested adults. Children's trails are available from the Information Desk.

VISITORS WITH DISABILITIES Limited car parking is available at the main entrance if booked in advance. Wheelchairs can be borrowed at both entrances, and lifts give access to the upper galleries. accessible lavatories are located off rooms 25 and 28 on the ground floor. The Lecture Theatre has an induction loop. If you need help in the Museum, please ask a warder or the Information Desk staff. For information about other services for visually handicapped and hearing impaired visitors, contact the Education Service on extn 8511.

PHOTOGRAPHY AND FILMING Photography, filming and video-recording in the galleries is permitted except where otherwise indicated, using hand-held equipment. Flash and monopods may be used. Permission must be obtained in advance for the use of any other equipment (including a tripod) and for commercial photography or filming. Please enquire at the Information Desk for details.

PHOTOGRAPHIC SERVICES Prints, slides and transparencies of objects in the Museum collections may be ordered. Price lists and further details from the Photographic Service or Information Desk.

PUBLICATIONS AND SHOPS British Museum Publications produces a wide range of books, including guides, exhibition catalogues, general books and scholarly monographs, as well as gift items such as replicas, jewellery, textiles, posters and postcards, which are on sale in the Museum shops. A mail order catalogue is available from 46 Bloomsbury Street, London WC1B 3QQ.

STUDENTS' ROOMS Admission is given by prior arrangement. However, staff are available to give opinions on objects related to the Museum collections as follows:

Coins and Medals
Western Asiatic
Mon-Fri 2-4.30, Sat 10-12.30

Egyptian
Greek and Roman
Prehistoric and Romano-British
Medieval and Later
Mon-Fri 2-4.30

Prints and Drawings
Mon-Fri 2.15-4

Oriental
Mon-Fri 2.15-4

Japanese
By appointment only

No valuations can be given.

TEMPORARY EXHIBITIONS The Museum presents a series of exhibitions on subjects related to the permanent collections. For some of these an admission charge is made. An exhibition programme is available from the Information Desk.

The Museum of Mankind

(The Ethnography Department of the British Museum)
6 Burlington Gardens
London W1X 2EX

OPENING HOURS As for the British Museum. The Museum of Mankind presents a series of regularly changing exhibitions illustrating a variety of non-Western cultures and societies. Ask at the Information Desk for an exhibition programme.

EDUCATION As at the British Museum, but the Museum of Mankind also offers some handling and demonstration sessions for school parties, and there is a lunch room which can be booked in advance.

PHOTOGRAPHY AND FILMING As at the British Museum.

PUBLICATIONS AND SHOP A wide range of books and gift items, as at the British Museum, is available from the Museum of Mankind Shop.

STUDENTS' ROOMS Admission is by prior arrangement. However, staff are available to give opinions Mon–Fri 1 – 4.45. Appointments are advisable and no valuations can be given.

PHOTOGRAPHIC ACKNOWLEDGEMENTS

All the photographs are by the British Museum Photographic Service, except the following: pp.4(left), 11, 12(top), 17(left), 25(buckle and purse-lid) and 29 (bottom) are by Lee Boltin, and p.26(right) is by the Hebridean Press Service, Stornaway.

©1989 The Trustees of the British Museum
Published by British Museum Publications Ltd
46 Bloomsbury Street, London WC1B 3QQ

ISBN 0-7141-1692-0

Designed by Roger Davies

Typeset by M&B. (Felsted) Ltd
Printed in Great Britain
BPC Paulton Books Ltd
Fourth Impression 1994